Birds of a Feather

QUILT PATTERN BY PIECE O' CAKE DESIGNS

Becky Goldsmith and Linda Jenkins

Made by Linda Jenkins

FINISHED QUILT: 37½″ × 37½″

BLOCKS: 10″ × 10″ · **SASHING SQUARES:** 1″ × 1″

INNER BORDERS: 1″-wide · **OUTER BORDERS:** 6¼″-wide

C&T PUBLISHING
Another Maker Inspired!

Publisher: Amy Barrett-Daffin

Creative Director: Gailen Runge

Senior Editor: Roxane Cerda

Editor: Liz Aneloski and Gailen Runge

Technical Editor: Debbie Rodgers

Designer: April Mostek

Production Coordinator: Zinnia Heinzmann

Illustrator: Becky Goldsmith

Photography Coordinator: Rachel Ackley

Instructional Photography by Becky Goldsmith

Quilt Photography by C&T Publishing, Inc.

Published by C&T Publishing, Inc., P.O. Box 1456, Lafayette, CA 94549

POD Edition

Contents

INTRODUCTION 4

FABRIC AND SUPPLIES 4

Choose Your Fabric 4

Fabric Preparation 4

Fabric Requirements 4

Cutting Instructions 4

Basic Appliqué Supplies 5

GENERAL INSTRUCTIONS 5

Prepare the Patterns 5

Audition Your Appliqué Blocks 6

Seam Allowances 6

GENERAL APPLIQUÉ INSTRUCTIONS 6

Appliqué Templates 6

Make Placement Overlays 7

Prepare the Background Blocks 7

Prepare Shapes for Needle-Turn Hand Appliqué 8

Prepare Shapes for Fusible Appliqué 8

Prepare the Long Bias Vine 8

Use the Placement Overlay to Position Appliqué Shapes 9

Use the Placement Overlay to Position the Border Vine 9

STITCHING OPTIONS 9

Needle-Turn Hand Appliqué 9

Fusible Appliqué 10

Wool Appliqué 10

Embroider the Blocks 10

QUILT ASSEMBLY AND FINISHING 10

Trim the Appliqué Blocks 10

Trim the Appliqué Borders 10

Assemble the Sashing Strips 10

Assemble the Quilt Top 10

Layer, Baste, and Quilt 12

Straight-Grain Binding 12

Construct and Attach a Hanging Sleeve 12

Document Your Quilt 12

BLOCK AND BORDER PATTERNS 13

Bird Block 1 13

Bird Block 2 15

Bird Block 3 17

Bird Block 4 19

Top and Bottom Border 21

Side Border 25

TEMPLATES 28

Templates for Bird Block 1 28

Templates for Bird Block 2 29

Templates for Bird Block 3 30

Templates for Bird Block 4 32

Templates for the Borders 34

ABOUT THE AUTHORS 35

INTRODUCTION • This quilt is a combination of five blocks (Blocks 50, 52, 53, and 55 and Border Block 104) from our book, *100 Whimsical Appliqué Designs*.

The four bird blocks are originally from our book, *Whimsical Quilt Garden*. The border was originally in our book, *Aunt Millie's Garden*. They are perfect together in this quilt.

Fabric and Supplies

CHOOSE YOUR FABRIC

Choose a variety of fabrics from your stash, go shopping, or both! Choose colors that make you smile. You will be handling them a lot so the more you love them, the happier you will be. You may not use every fabric that you begin with—and you can always add more to the mix.

FABRIC PREPARATION

- Cotton fabric shrinks, and you can't tell by look or feel how much an individual fabric might shrink.
- Fabric dyes can bleed when wet. Water chemistry, which varies from place to place, has an impact on dye migration.
- Fabric off-the-bolt has been treated with a wide array of chemicals that cause allergic reactions in some people.
- We always wash fabric in the washer and dry it in the dryer before using it to remove excess dyes and chemicals and to shrink it to its final size. We don't add any "spray" products to fabrics before using them. We press with steam and sometimes a spritz of water. Washed fabric feels and smells nice and it has a nap that helps to hold shapes in place as you pin and sew.

Fabric Requirements

Yardages are based on 40″-wide fabric (WOF).

BLOCK BACKGROUND

¾ yard

BORDER BACKGROUND

1⅛ yard

SASHING SQUARES

A variety of scraps, ¼ yard or more

INNER BORDER

¼ yard

APPLIQUÉ

Large scraps, fat quarters, or larger if you repeat fabrics

BIAS VINE

½ yard

BACKING AND SLEEVE

2⅔ yards

STRAIGHT BINDING

½ yard

BATTING

45″ × 45″

Cutting Instructions

BLOCK BACKGROUNDS

Cut 4 squares 12″ × 12″.

BORDER BACKGROUNDS

Cut 4 rectangles 8¼″ × WOF.

Subcut 2 rectangles 8¼″ × 27″ for the top and bottom borders.

Subcut 2 rectangles 8¼″ × 39½″ for the side borders.

SASHING SQUARES

Cut 129 squares 1½″ × 1½″.

INNER BORDER

Cut 4 rectangles 1½″ × WOF.

Subcut 2 rectangles 1½″ × 23½″ for the side borders.

Subcut 2 rectangles 1½″ × 25½″ for the top and bottom borders.

APPLIQUÉ

Use templates and cut as desired. Refer to Prepare the Long Bias Vine (page 8) for more details on the border appliqué.

BINDING

Cut 5 strips 2½″ by WOF.

Basic Appliqué Supplies

- 8½″ × 11″ plain paper, *English Paper-Piecing Specialty Paper* (C&T Publishing), or smooth white 60–65lb cardstock for templates: approximately 7 sheets
- 9″ × 12″ Single-sided self-adhesive laminate sheets: approximately 7 sheets
- Medium-weight, clear vinyl for the placement overlay:

  ¾ yard if 60″-wide

  OR 2 packages with one 16″ × 1½ yards of 12-gauge vinyl each (we use *Premium Clear Vinyl,* C&T Publishing)
- A black ultra fine point permanent marker (we use Sharpie Ultra Fine Point markers.) for the placement overlay
- Karen Kay Buckley's Perfect Stems bias bars tool
- Scissors: small, sharp scissors for paper and for fabric. I recommend serrated scissors for fabric because they hold and control the fabric as when you cut.
- Marking Tools: The goal is to make marks that you can see but that do not show on the finished quilt top. I use a firm graphite pencil on light fabric and white chalk pencil on medium to dark fabric. No matter which pencils you choose, it is a good idea to test them on fabric before you begin.
- Pins for appliqué and piecing
- Thread for appliqué and piecing. If you'd like to know more about thread, please refer to the book, *The Ultimate Thread Guide*, by Becky Goldsmith.
- Optional: Sandpaper board to keep fabric from shifting as you trace around it.

If you choose hand appliqué:

- Hand sewing needles
- Thimble(s)

If you choose fusible appliqué:

- Fusible Web: We recommend Wonder Fuse by Clover.
- Teflon pressing sheet to use with fusible web

General Instructions

PREPARE THE PATTERNS

Print or copy the pattern pages at actual size. Check the 1″ × 1″ square and if the size is not correct, check your printer settings.

Trim the pattern pages and tape them together to make the full-size pattern. Use a ruler to keep lines straight.

Full-Size Patterns

Full-size patterns for copyshop printing are available by visiting this tiny url: **tinyurl.com/60507-patterns-download**

PREPARE THE BORDER PATTERNS

1. Print the Border pattern pages.
2. Trim the Side Border pages and tape them together to make the full-size patterns. Use a ruler to keep center lines straight.
3. Repeat for the Top and Bottom Borders.

AUDITION YOUR APPLIQUÉ BLOCKS

In the same way that an actor auditions for a part, fabric should audition for its place in your quilt. Every individual piece of fabric has an impact on all the other pieces of fabric. If possible, use a design wall big enough to accommodate your quilt top.

Place all the backgrounds and all appliqué shapes on the wall. It is also good to get your sashing squares and inner border strips up on the wall if that's possible. Play with your choices until you are happy with your quilt. Take a photo of your quilt on the design wall for reference.

SEAM ALLOWANCES

A 3⁄16˝ seam allowance is perfect for needle-turn hand appliqué. Less than that can cause the raw edges to fray; more can cause the seam allowance to bunch up.

When appliqué shapes overlap, the seam allowance that falls underneath can be cut a little bigger.

Use a ¼˝ seam allowance when piecing the quilt together.

Quilt in progress on the design wall.

General Appliqué Instructions

Refer to the book, *The Best-Ever Appliqué Sampler*, by Becky Goldsmith and Linda Jenkins (C&T Publishing), and/or *Hand Sewing*, by Becky Goldsmith (C&T Publishing), for more detailed appliqué instructions.

APPLIQUÉ TEMPLATES

Appliqué templates are the finished size of the shape—no seam allowances are added. Keep the shapes for each block together. Each appliqué shape requires its own template. When shapes overlap, you will need a template for each of those shapes.

1. Print the template pages onto plain paper, *English Paper-Piecing Specialty Paper* (C&T Publishing), or white card stock.

2. Trim the pages as needed and tape them together. Tape both the front and back sides of the join.

3. Cover the template shapes with single-sided self-adhesive laminating sheets. Overlap the edges of the laminate on top of the templates. Cover all template shapes.

4. Cut out each template, splitting the drawn line with your scissors. Do not cut outside of the lines as it adds to the size of the template. Keep edges smooth and points sharp.

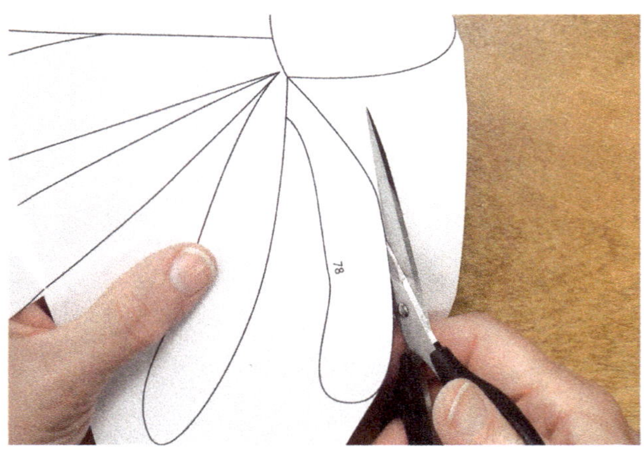

MAKE PLACEMENT OVERLAYS

The placement overlay allows you to accurately position your shapes on the block without tracing on your background fabric or the need to use a lightbox.

1. Cut a piece of clear, medium-weight vinyl to the finished size of the blocks and borders.

4 squares 10″ × 10″ for the Bird blocks

6¼″ × 25″ rectangle for the Top and Bottom Border

6¼″ × 37½″ rectangle for the Side Border

2. Working with one pattern at a time, tape the pattern onto a table to keep it from shifting out of place. Tape the clear vinyl over the pattern.

3. Use a black ultra fine point permanent marker to draw the horizontal and vertical center lines onto the vinyl. Draw an "X" in the upper right-hand corner of the overlay.

4. Trace the pattern and the numbers onto the vinyl. If your pen goes off the line, just pick it up and move it back in place. You won't be graded on how well you trace. :-)

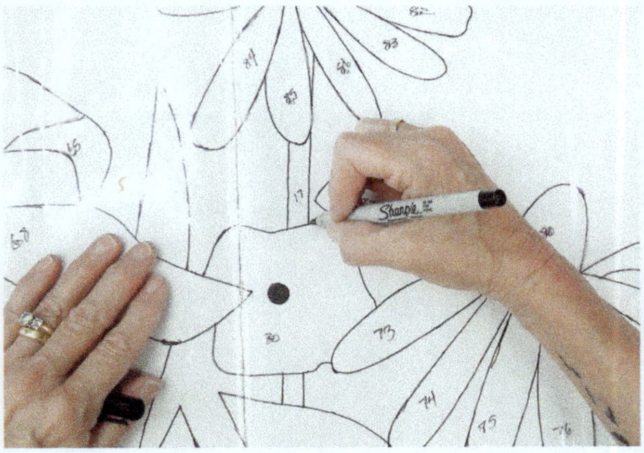

PREPARE THE BACKGROUND BLOCKS

1. Cut backgrounds as directed (page 4).

2. Press the block and border backgrounds in half, horizontally and vertically. The pressed-in grid aligns with the drawn center grid on the placement overlay.

3. Draw a short line on each end of the pressed-in lines at the raw edges of the fabric. These short lines help when you position the placement overlay on the block.

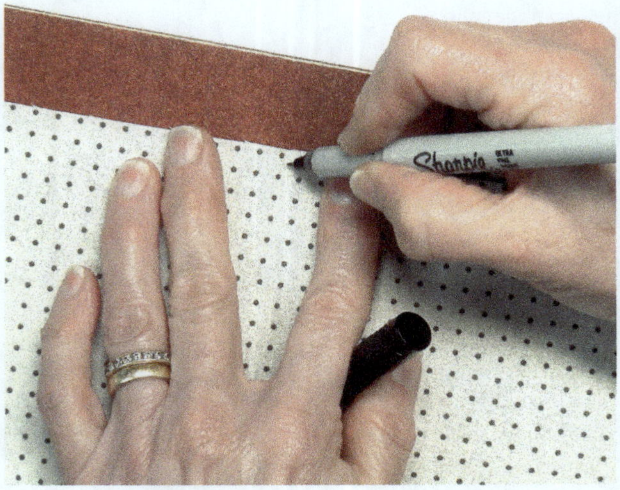

4. Draw an "X" in the upper right-hand corner of the background in the excess fabric that will be trimmed away after your aplliqué is complete. Number your Bird block backgrounds in the excess fabric in the upper right-hand corner as well. Make a "map" to help you get the blocks back into position before setting the quilt together.

If your backgrounds are directional, you may want to add additional notations on the background or on a note attached to the block.

PREPARE SHAPES FOR NEEDLE-TURN HAND APPLIQUÉ

1. Place the appliqué fabric right-side up on a sandpaper board. The sandpaper keeps the fabric from shifting as you trace around the fabric. If you do not have a sandpaper board, try using your rotary cutting mat.

2. Place the template right-side up on the fabric. Turn the template so that most edges are on the bias grain of the fabric unless you are fussy-cutting the shape to take advantage of a design in the fabric.

3. Trace around the shape, making a line you can see.

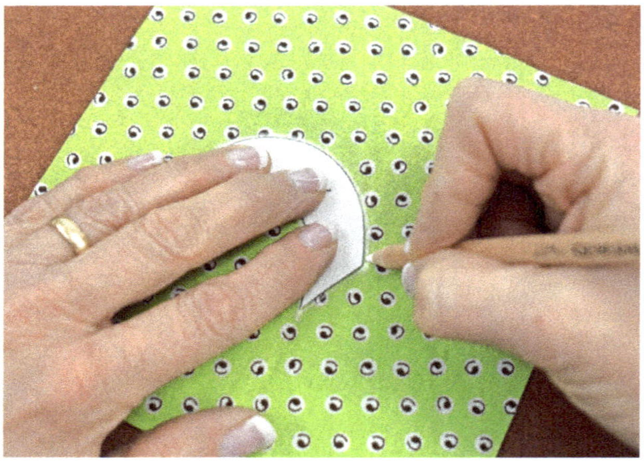

4. Cut the shape out, leaving a 3⁄16˝ seam allowance. You can cut a slightly larger seam allowance on edges that lie underneath another appliqué shape.

PREPARE SHAPES FOR FUSIBLE APPLIQUÉ

Follow the directions on the fusible web.

1. Turn templates upside-down on the paper side of the fusible product. Trace around the shapes.

2. Cut the shapes out leaving a small margin of paper and fusible web around each shape.

3. Press the fusible web to the wrong side of the appliqué fabric. Use a teflon sheet to protect your iron and ironing surface.

4. Cut away the excess fabric around the shape. You can leave a little bit of seam allowance in places where one appliqué shape falls underneath another shape so that these edges overlap.

PREPARE THE LONG BIAS VINE

Treat stems 1–4 as regular appliqué shapes, using templates. The long vines in the border are a perfect place to use Karen Kay Buckley's Perfect Stems bias bars tool.

1. Cut 16 strips 1½˝-wide on the bias from the Bias Vine fabric.

2. Make a continuous bias strip 360˝ long.

3. Follow the instructions on the Perfect Stems package to make 3⁄16˝-wide stems.

Once made, the finished edges of these vines are ready to stitch.

USE THE PLACEMENT OVERLAY TO POSITION APPLIQUÉ SHAPES

1. Place the background block right side up on your sandboard, cutting mat, or on your ironing surface if you are fusing.

2. Place the overlay right side up over the background, lining up the centerlines.

3. Hold the overlay in place with one hand. Lift the edge of the overlay and slide the appliqué shape into place. Adjust as needed and then pin—or fuse if you are fusing—the shape in place.

4. Appliqué shapes in place.

USE THE PLACEMENT OVERLAY TO POSITION THE BORDER VINE

1. Place the border right-side up on a rotary cutting mat. Place the overlay on it, lining up the centerlines. You can use a few pins to help hold it in place.

2. Carefully lift one long side of the overlay and reach underneath to maneuver the vine into place. Work from one end to the other, pinning or gluing the overlay in place as you go. Be sure not to let the overlay shift.

3. Once the vine is pinned in place, take the time to baste it. Remove the pins, smooth out the curves, and baste it in place.

Stitching Options

Choose your favorite appliqué method. Refer to the book, *The Best-Ever Appliqué Sampler*, by Becky Goldsmith and Linda Jenkins, and/or *Hand Sewing*, by Becky Goldsmith, for more detailed appliqué instructions.

NEEDLE-TURN HAND APPLIQUÉ

Place your appliqué fabric right side up on a sandboard to keep the fabric from shifting. Place your template right side up on the fabric and trace around it. Cut shapes out adding a 3⁄16″ seam allowance.

Finger-press the seam allowance to the back of the appliqué shape before placing them on the block. You'll be amazed at how much easier this one step makes turning the seam allowance under.

Use the placement overlay to position shapes on the background. Pin or baste and then stitch each shape in place.

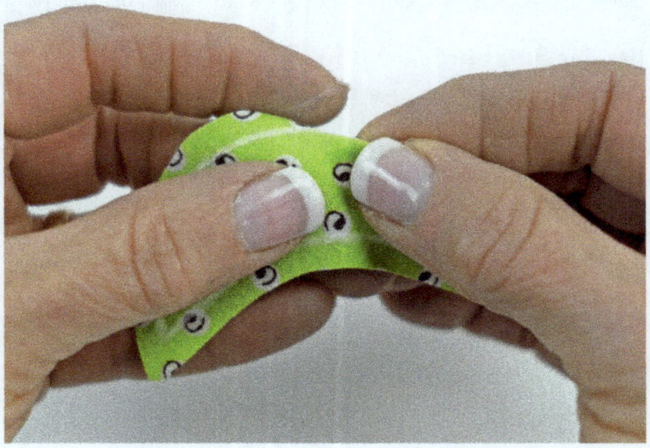

FUSIBLE APPLIQUÉ

Follow the directions on the package. Use a Teflon pressing sheet to protect the iron and the ironing surface. Do not overheat the fusible.

Raw edges can be finished by hand or machine with a blanket stitch, satin stitch, or any other stitch that suits you.

WOOL APPLIQUÉ

Felted wool and wool felt are lovely to appliqué with. We use Wonder Fuse by Clover to hold wool shapes in place on the block and to help stabilize the raw edges. You can also use pins, some glues, or basting.

Sew the edges of the appliqué with a whip stitch or blanket stitch. Wool thread in matching colors is more invisible. Perle cotton is showier depending on thread weight and color.

Wool appliqué looks great with embroidery—a little or a lot. :-)

EMBROIDER THE BLOCKS

Use a lightbox and trace the block design onto your background fabric. Embroider the outlines and fill the shapes with stitches of your choice. You can use only one color, like red or blue, or use a variety of colors.

You can also combine hand-sewn or fused appliqué shapes with embroidered areas!

Quilt Assembly and Finishing

TRIM THE APPLIQUÉ BLOCKS

1. Place the Bird blocks right-side down on your ironing surface and press them.
2. Trim the blocks to 10½″ × 10½″.

TRIM THE APPLIQUÉ BORDERS

1. Place the borders right-side down on your ironing surface and press them.
2. Trim the Top and Bottom borders to 6¾″ × 25½″.
3. Trim the Side borders to 6¾″ × 38″.

ASSEMBLE THE SASHING STRIPS

Sashing Strips A: Sew together 10 squares 1½″ × 1½″ to make 6 vertical strips. Press seam allowances in one direction.

Sashing Strips B: Sew together 23 squares 1½″ × 1½″ to make 3 horizontal strips. Press seam allowances in one direction.

ASSEMBLE THE QUILT TOP

1. Place the trimmed blocks, sashing strips, inner border strips, and borders on your design wall. Check the position of blocks and borders against the photo you took at the end of the audition process.
2. Sew the top 2 blocks together with 3 A sashing strips as shown in the Quilt Assembly Diagram. Press seam allowances toward the blocks. Repeat for the bottom 2 blocks.
3. Sew a B sashing strip to the top of the top row. Change the direction of the pressed seam allowances in the sashing strip as needed to nest the seams. Press seam allowances toward the blocks.
4. Sew a B sashing strip to the top and to the bottom of the bottom row. Change the direction of the pressed seam allowances in the sashing strips as needed to nest the seams. Press seam allowances toward the blocks.
5. Sew the rows together. Press seam allowances toward the blocks.
6. Sew the side inner border strips to the quilt. Press seam allowances toward the inner border.
7. Sew the top and bottom inner border strips to the quilt. Press seam allowances toward the inner border.
8. Sew the top and bottom borders to the quilt. Press seam allowances to the inner borders.
9. Sew the side borders to the quilt. Press seam allowances to the inner borders.

Quilt Assembly Diagram

LAYER, BASTE, AND QUILT

1. Layer the quilt back, batting, and quilt top. Be sure layers are centered and smooth.

2. Baste the layers together.

3. Quilt by hand or machine.

STRAIGHT-GRAIN BINDING

1. Trim away the selvages and cut the ends of the strips at the same 45° angle.

2. Sew the strips together end-to-end.

3. Press the binding in half wrong sides together, lengthwise.

4. If you have a walking foot, attach it to your sewing machine and sew the binding to the quilt, using a ¼˝ seam allowance. Sew binding to all edges and join the ends.

5. Fold binding toward the quilt back to cover the raw edges of the batting and backing.

6. Hand stitch the binding to the back of the quilt.

CONSTRUCT AND ATTACH A HANGING SLEEVE

Placing a hanging sleeve on your quilt ensures that it will never be nailed to the wall.

1. Cut or construct a strip 8½˝ × the width of your quilt. Adjust the length so that, once hemmed, it will be about 2˝ narrower than the bound quilt.

2. Turn under ½˝ twice, press, and hem the short ends of the strip with matching thread.

3. Fold the strip in half wrong sides together, lengthwise. Match the raw edges and sew the sleeve strip into a tube.

4. Place the sleeve on your ironing board with the seam centered. Press the seam allowance open and the sleeve flat.

5. With the sleeve right side up on your ironing board, press an additional lengthwise crease ½˝ away from the fold at the bottom of the sleeve. This creates a little fullness in the sleeve to accommodate the thickness of the rod.

6. Center the top edge of the sleeve on the top, back of your quilt with the seam allowances hidden between the sleeve and quilt back. Pin or baste the top edge in place.

7. With the sleeve flat, lift the top layer of the sleeve to expose the third crease. Pin or baste the sleeve in place along this crease.

8. Hand sew the sleeve to the back of the quilt.

DOCUMENT YOUR QUILT

The people who will own your quilt in the future will want to know about this quilt! Always make and attach a documentation patch and include your name and any details you choose to share.

Documentation patches can be computer generated, embroidered, or handwritten with a permanent fabric pen. Add appliqué, photo transfers—whatever seems right to you.

Include your name, location, and the date. Your quilt may need to be washed so include the fiber content. Share the name of the pattern you used. If you made the quilt for a special person or occasion, be sure to include that as well.

1. Make a label for your quilt.

2. Hem the edges of the label.

3. Hand stitch the label to the back of your quilt.

Block and Border Patterns

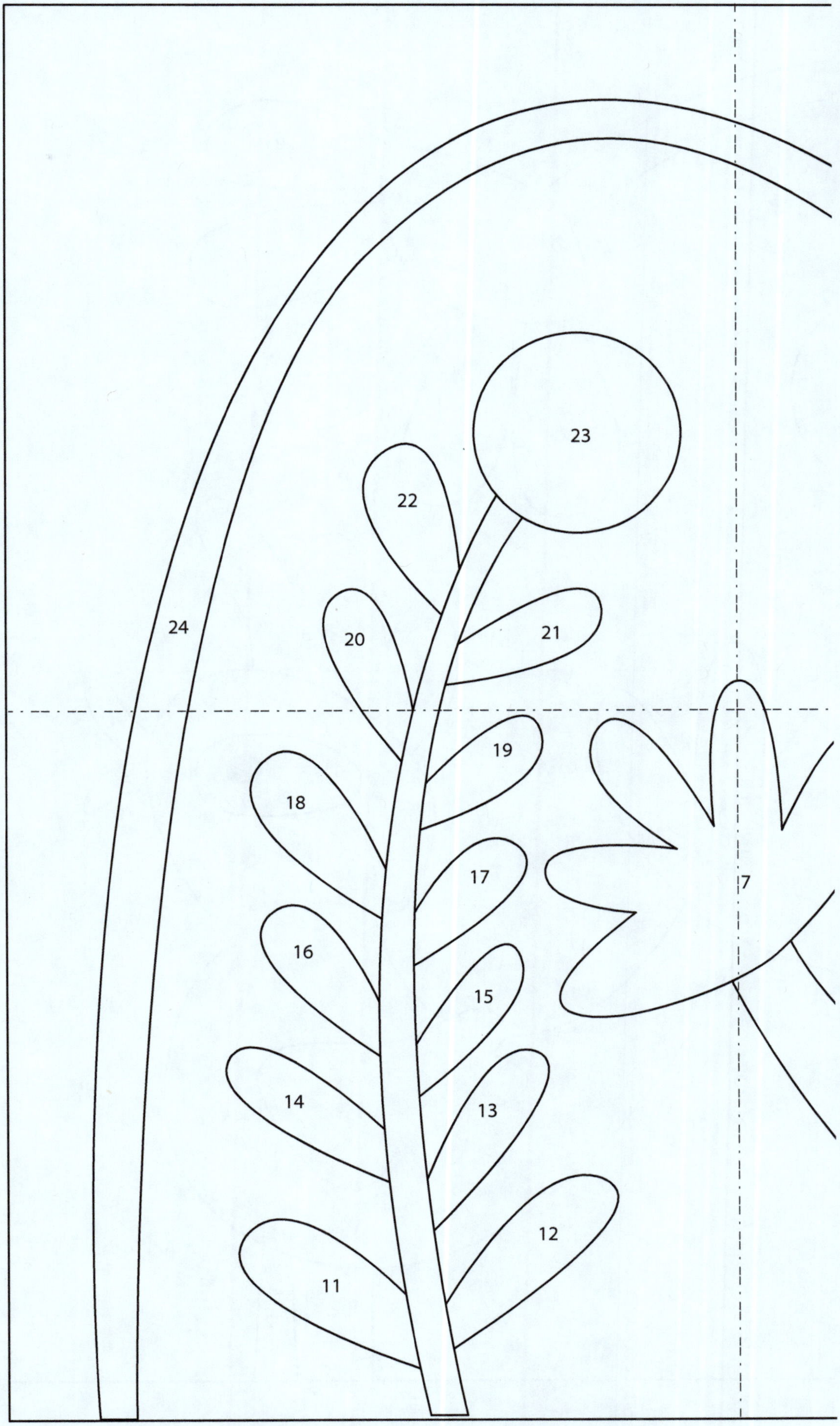

To make complete pattern, join the pages, following the diagram for reference.

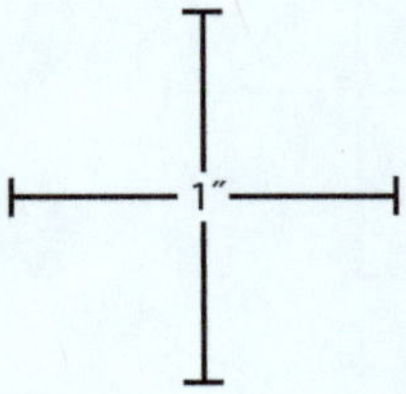

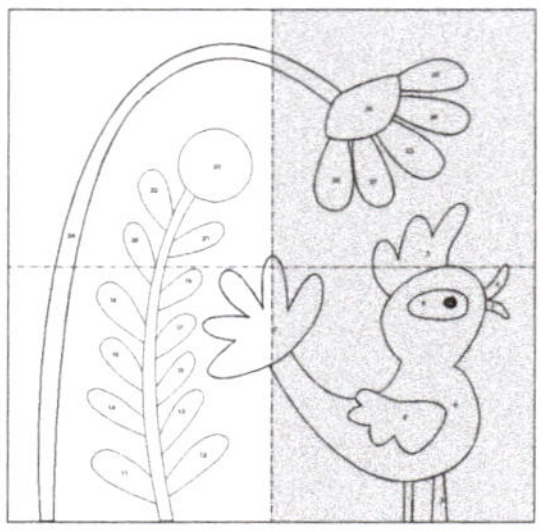

To make complete pattern, join the pages, following the diagram for reference.

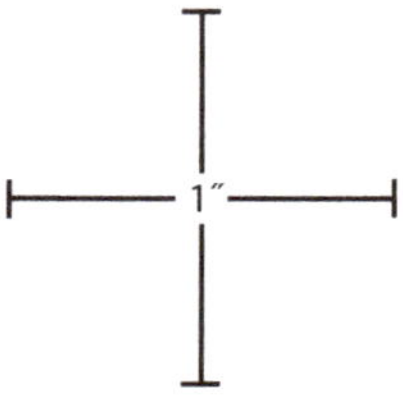

To make complete pattern, join the pages, following the diagram for reference.

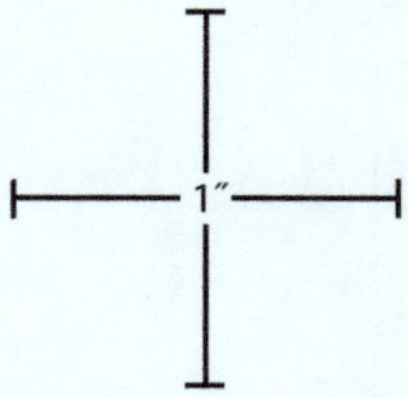

To make complete pattern, join the pages, following the diagram for reference.

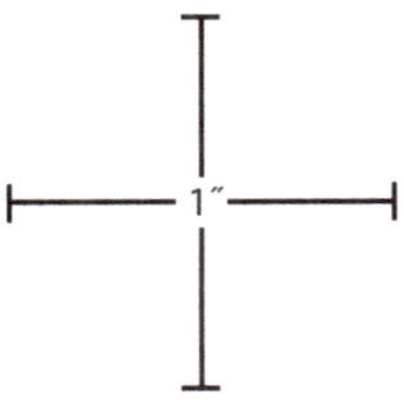

To make complete pattern, join the pages, following the diagram for reference.

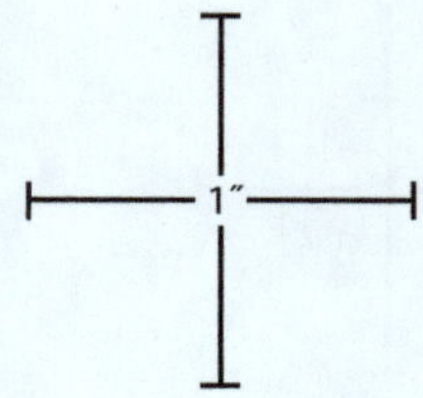

To make complete pattern, join the pages, following the diagram for reference.

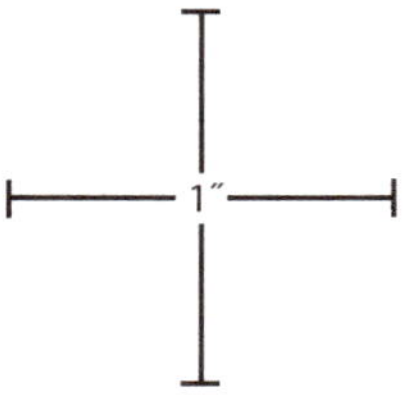

To make complete pattern, join the pages, following the diagram for reference.

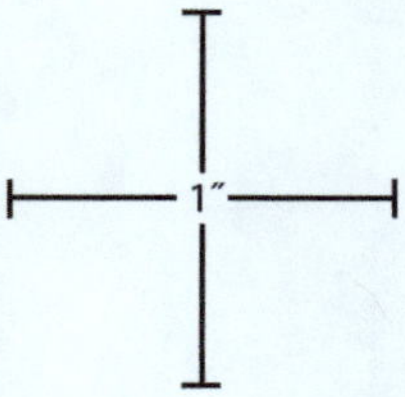

To make complete pattern, join the pages, following the diagram for reference.

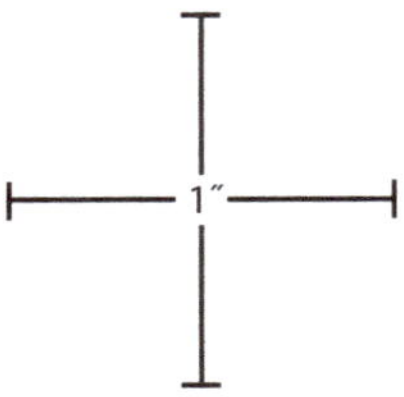

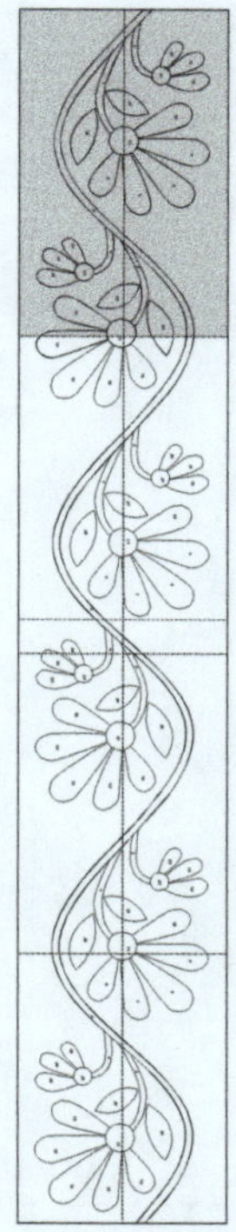

To make complete pattern, join the pages, following the diagram for reference.

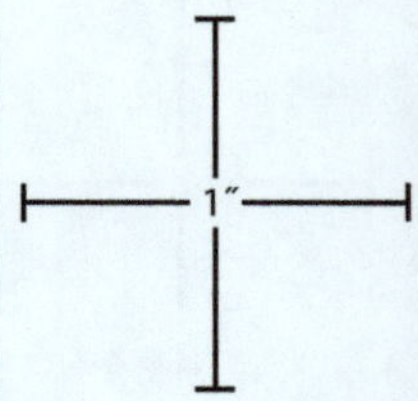

To make complete pattern, join the pages, following the diagram for reference.

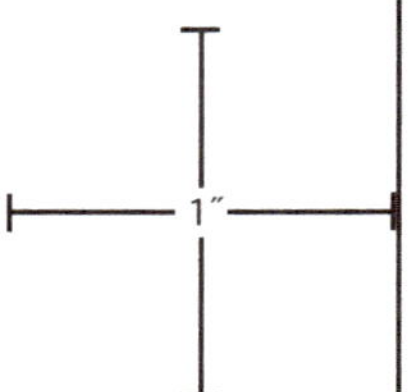

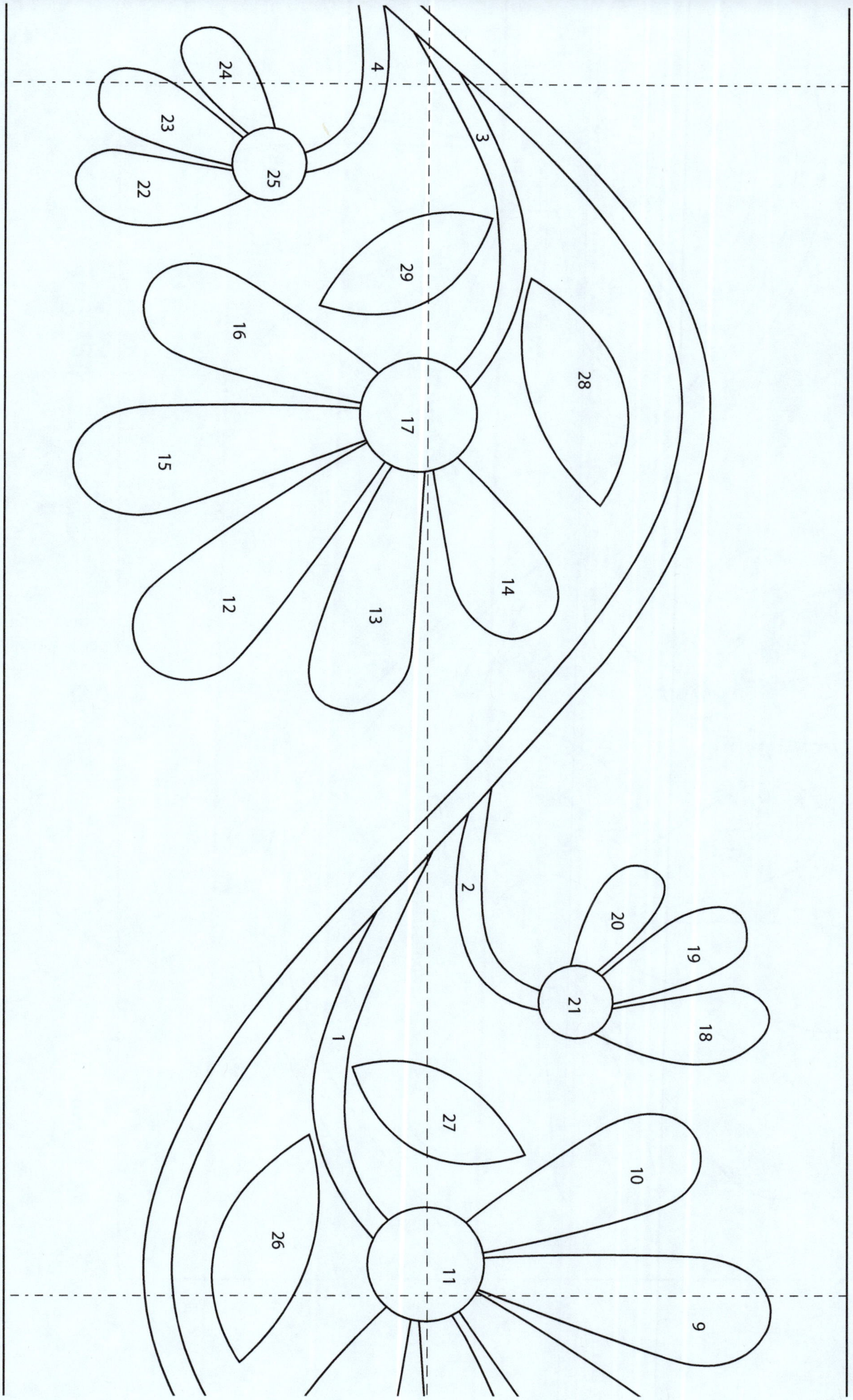

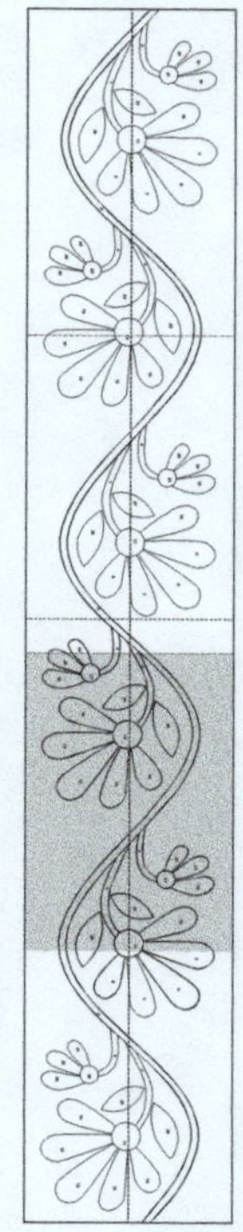

To make complete pattern, join the pages, following the diagram for reference.

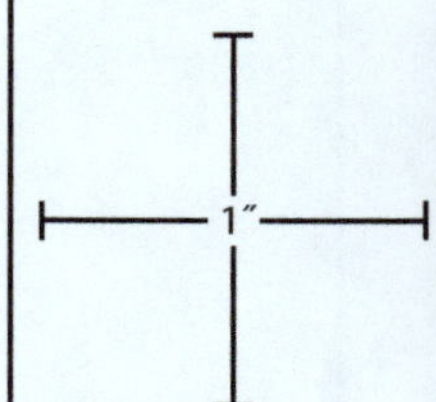

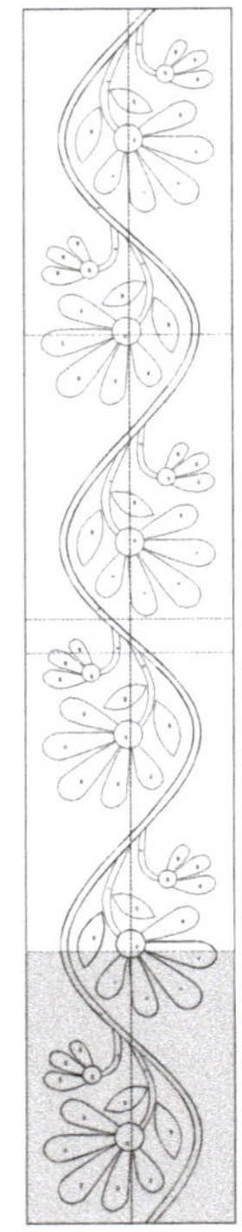

To make complete pattern, join the pages, following the diagram for reference.

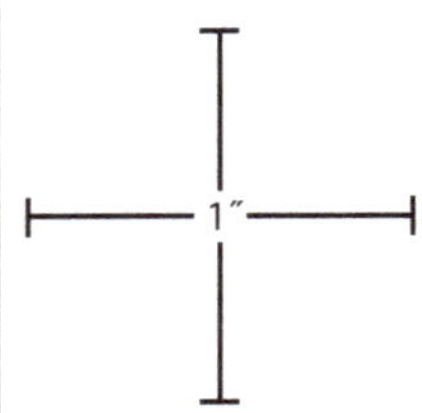

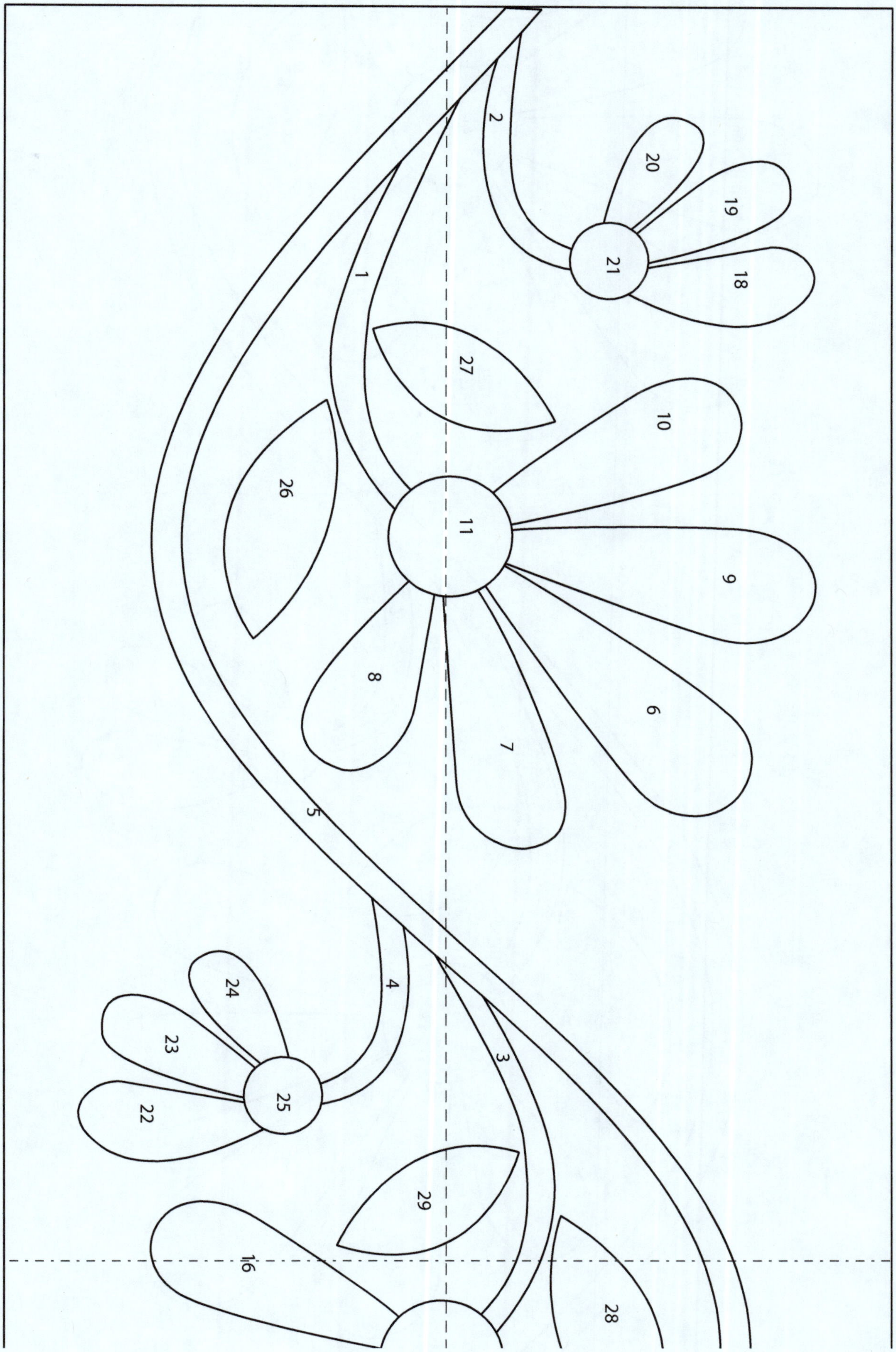

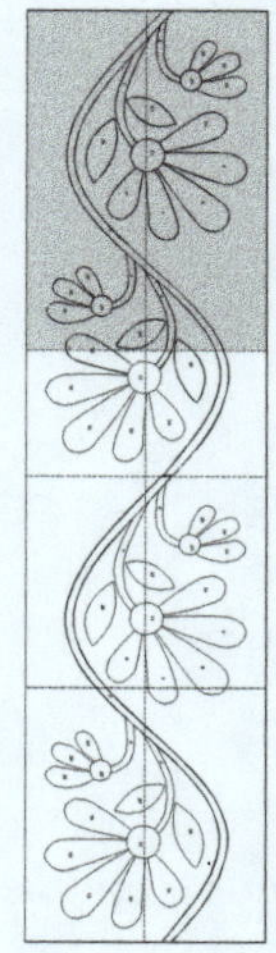

To make complete pattern, join the pages, following the diagram for reference.

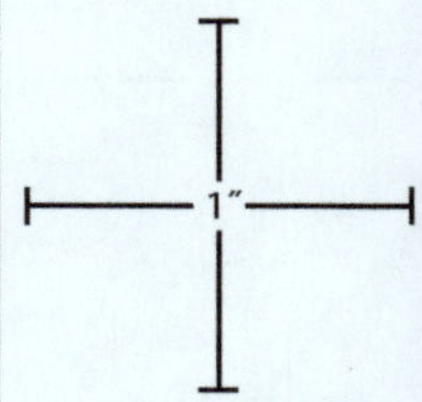

To make complete pattern, join the pages, following the diagram for reference.

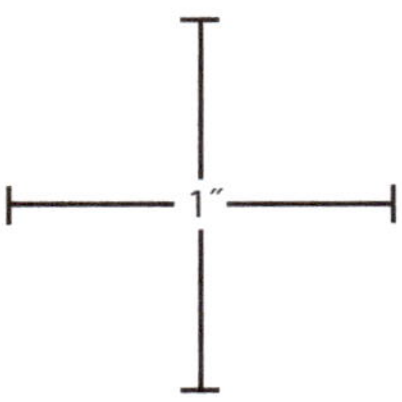

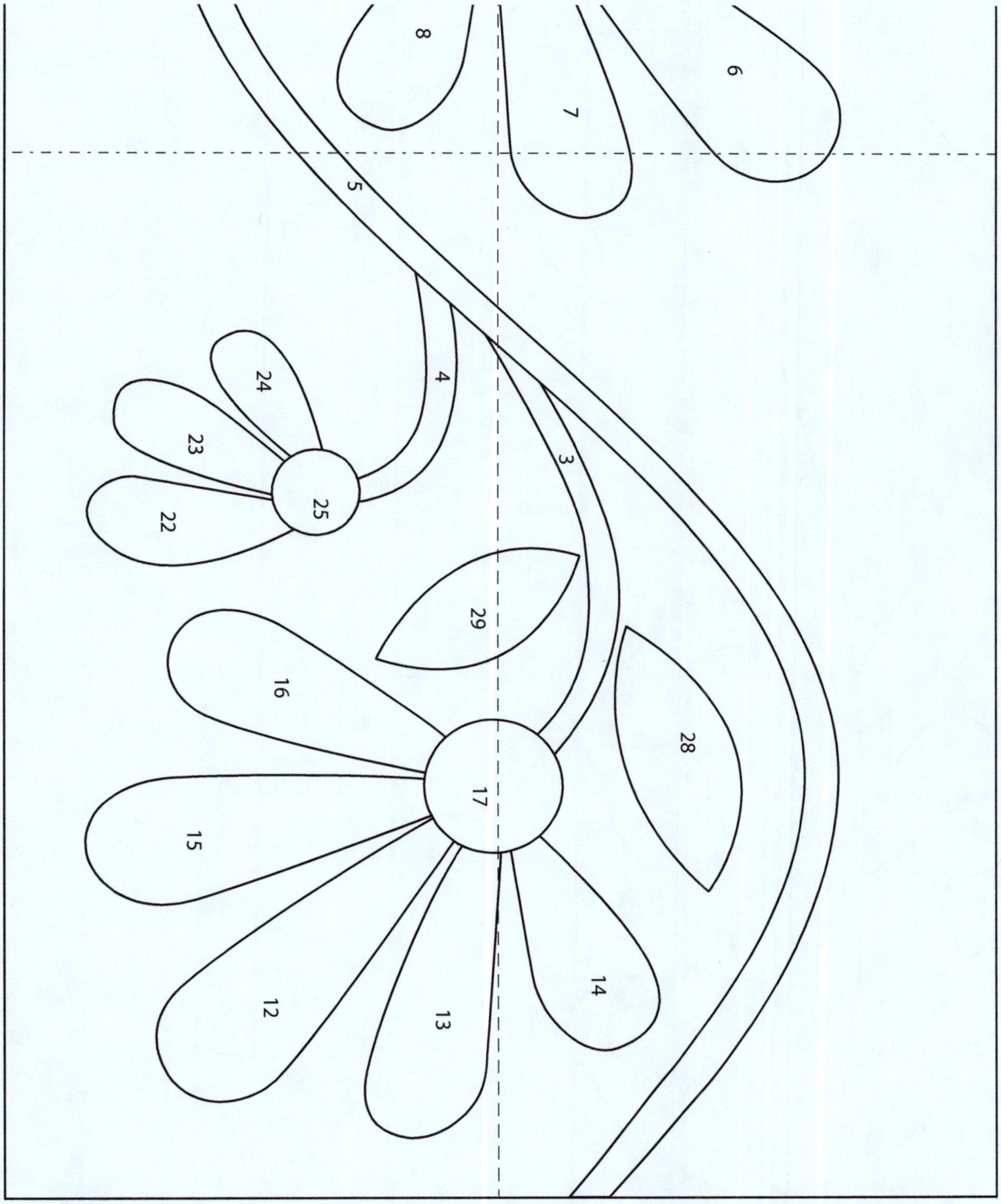

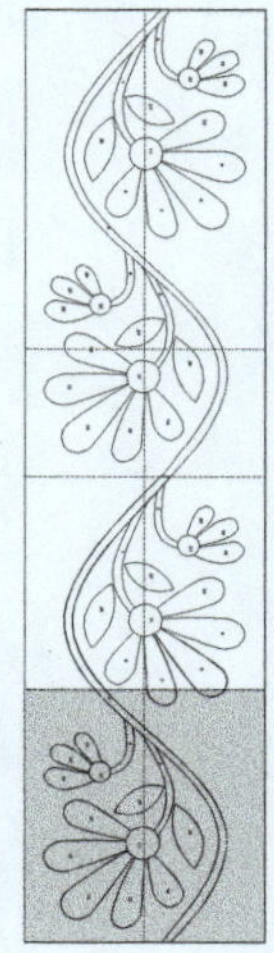

To make complete pattern, join the pages, following the diagram for reference.

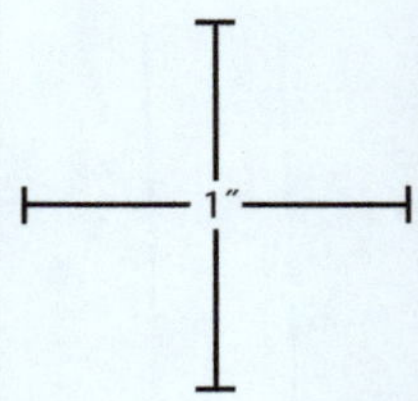

Templates

Templates for Bird Block 1

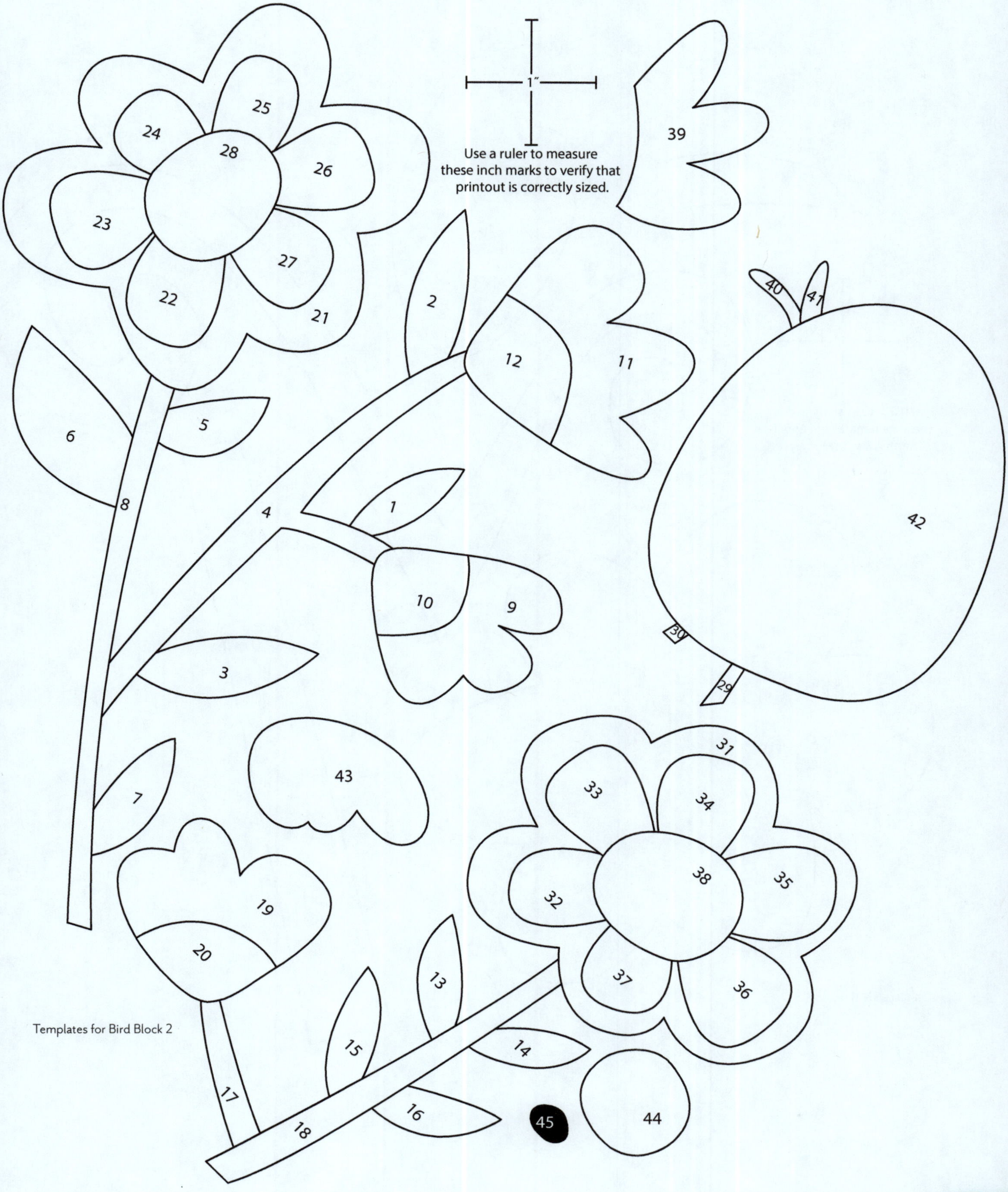

Templates for Bird Block 2

Use a ruler to measure these inch marks to verify that printout is correctly sized.

Templates for Bird Block 3

Use a ruler to measure these inch marks to verify that printout is correctly sized.

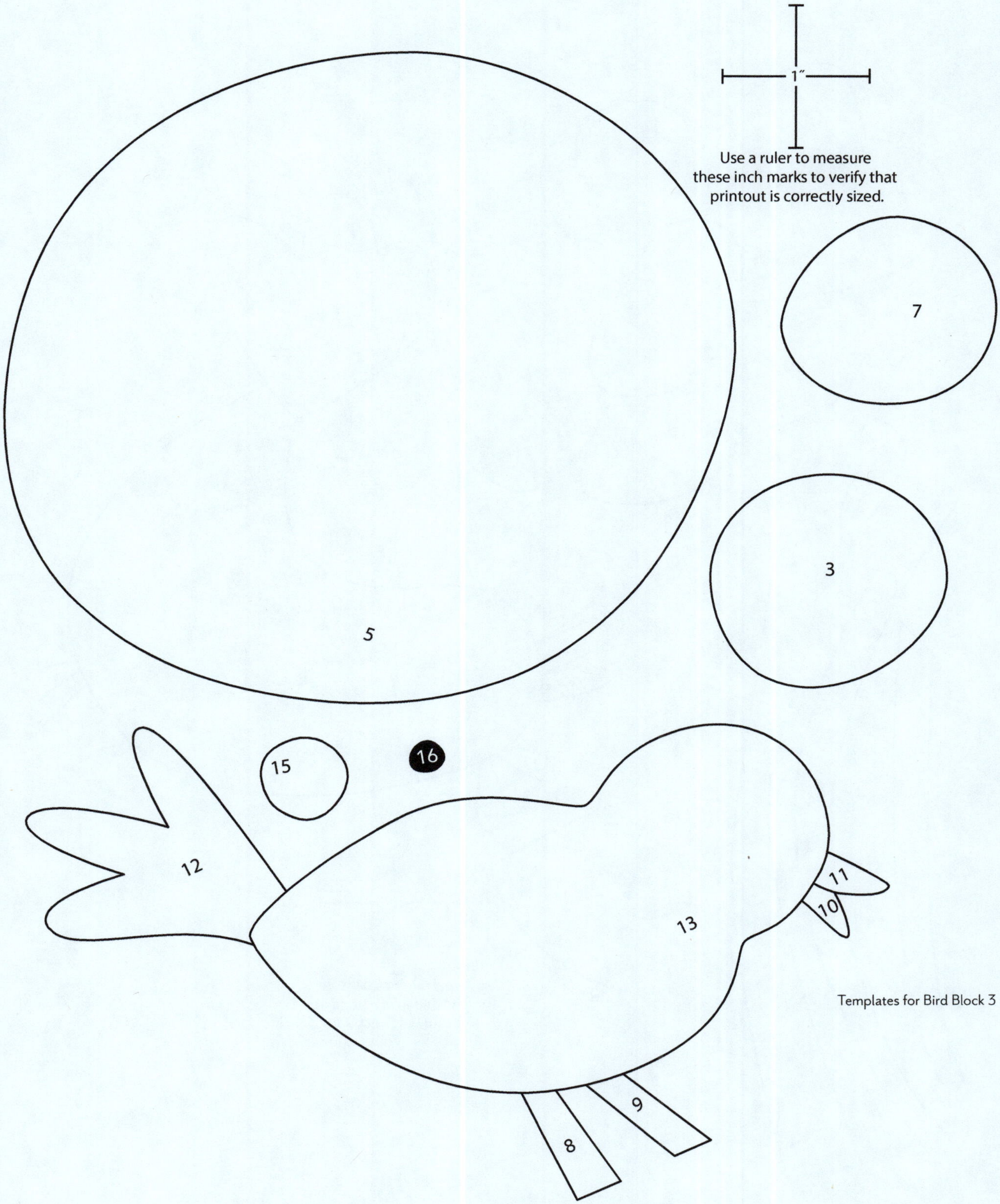

Templates for Bird Block 3

Use a ruler to measure these inch marks to verify that printout is correctly sized.

Templates for Bird Block 4

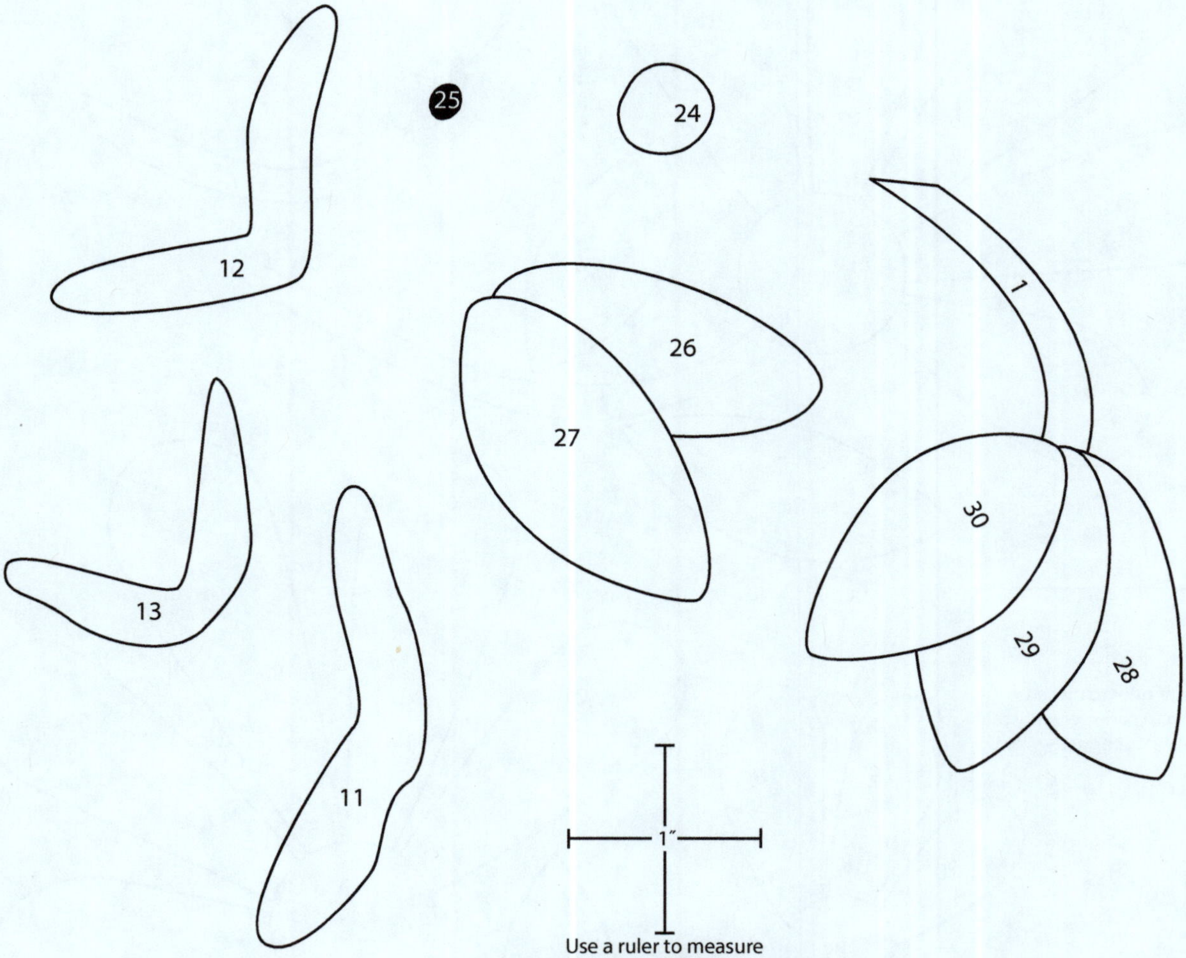

Use a ruler to measure
these inch marks to verify that
printout is correctly sized.

Templates for Bird Block 4

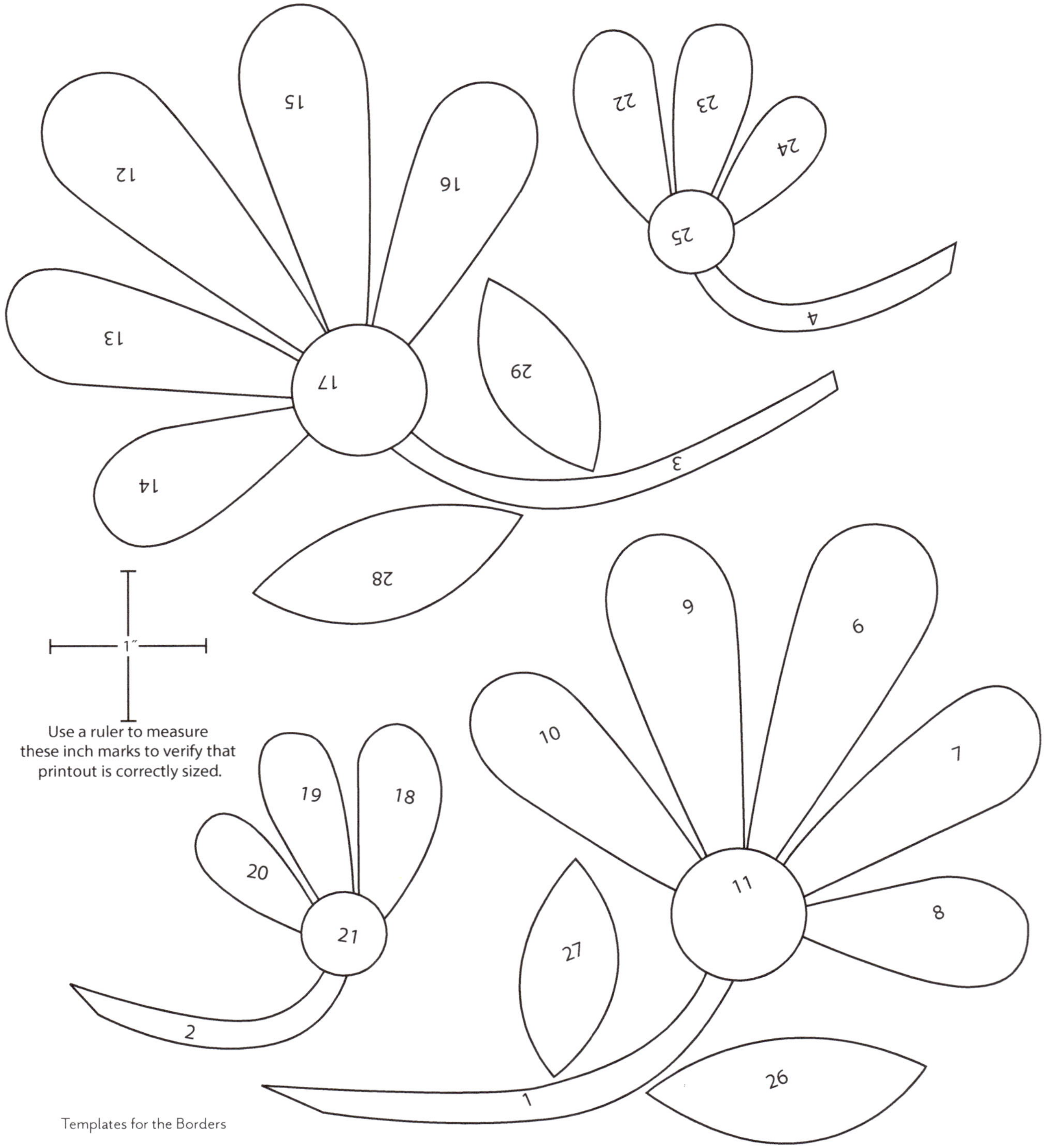

Use a ruler to measure these inch marks to verify that printout is correctly sized.

Templates for the Borders

About the Authors

Becky Goldsmith

Linda Jenkins

BECKY GOLDSMITH and **LINDA JENKINS** met and became best friends forever at the Green Country Quilters Guild in Tulsa, OK. They started Piece O' Cake Designs in 1994 and, over the years, produced so many books and patterns that they have lost track of the number.

Linda retired from the business in 2014, but she is still appliquéing and giving Becky suggestions about what books and patterns ought to come next. :-) Linda took an active part in putting together their most recent book and this series of patterns and made several of the quilts.

Becky continues to write and publish new books and patterns under her own name and as Piece O' Cake. She teaches online and has a variety of online courses on Creative Spark Online Learning. You can find Becky on Instagram **@beckygoldsmith**, and on Facebook.

Find Piece O' Cake online at **pieceocake.com**

Other patterns by Piece O' Cake

Other titles by Piece O' Cake

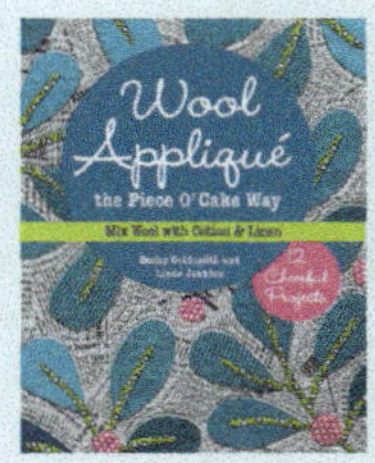

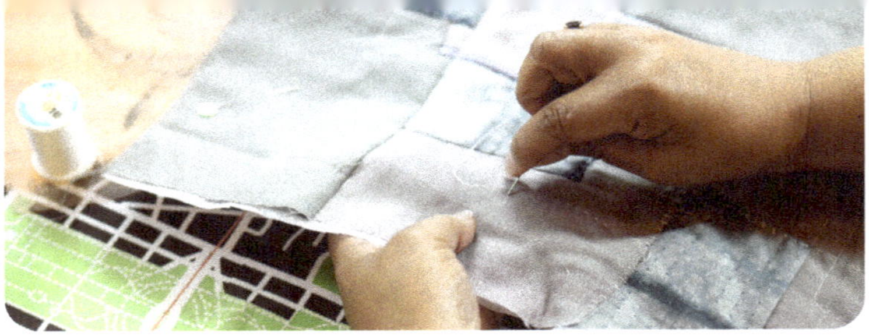

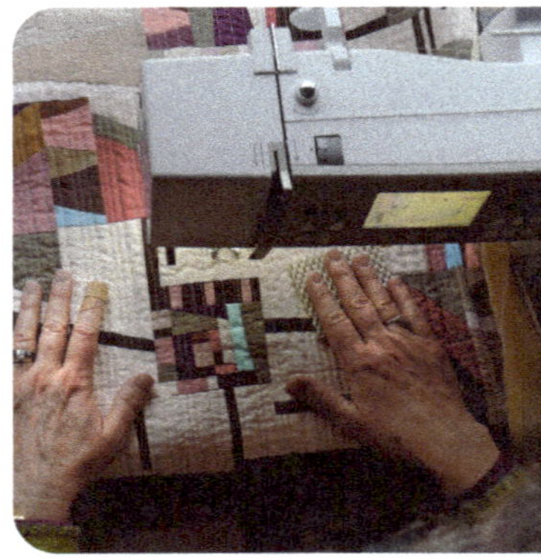

www.ingramcontent.com/pod-product-compliance
Lightning Source LLC
LaVergne TN
LVHW071208250826
R19618000002B/R196180PG846228LVX00002B/1
* 9 7 8 1 6 4 4 0 3 5 7 4 0 *